The Plumtree Diaries

By
Gordon Wallis

CONTENTS

CHAPTER ONE

The Build-Up

I suppose it was around 1984. I was 14 or 15 years old and was attending a school in Harare, Zimbabwe, by the name of Oriel Boy's High. I was in the second form which meant I had been in secondary school for two years already. Standards at the school were low - only getting worse and being day scholars, we were subject to many distractions after hours. The most popular of these distractions was the local ice cream parlour by the name of Dairy Den. There were two vintage video game consoles there. Pac-man and Donkey Kong. Apart from the choc crunchie dip 99 cones, these games were the sole focus of a small group of friends and me. In those days it was common for boys to cycle to school and thus we had our own transport, so in the afternoons after school we would congregate there to spend whatever money we had acquired on games, cigarettes and ice cream.

They were happy carefree days, but our grades were suffering and our parents had decided that a change was in order. Towards the end of that current school year my parents announced that my younger brother and I would be going to boarding school the following term. The very fact that it was to be a boarding school was enough to upset us deeply, but it was the name of said boarding school that struck terror into our hearts. It was to be a school far away from our home in Harare. A school in the south of Zimbabwe on the border with Botswana. A school with a fearsome reputation for discipline and tradition. A school by the name of Plumtree. My brother and I took the news with shock, but my parents wasted no time and took us on an outing to buy our new uniforms and other items that students at boarding schools would need. My younger brother was more accepting of his fate, but I could personally think of nothing worse. The thought of being trapped in what was effectively a military academy, hundreds of kilometres from home in a completely unknown and new environment was terrifying. Then there were the rumours.

Rumours of punishing rules, harsh discipline and strict seniority were heard often and these only added to my sense of impending doom along with the feelings of disquiet. One consolation was the fact that my younger brother and a friend of mine from Oriel, Bailey, were to accompany me, but even this was not enough to placate the deep fear that I felt. With our uniforms and sports kit purchased, the last things on the long list of items we would need were our trunks. Made from pressed sheet metal and sprayed black with a clasp for a padlock, they were painted in bold white letters with our names by a sign writer. I guess it was when these trunks were being packed with our belongings that it really hit home. I was going to Plumtree and there was nothing I could do about it. Or was there?

CHAPTER TWO

The Runaways

It was roughly three weeks before the dreaded date I was due to leave that I and two friends, Buckley and Mann, decided we would go and watch a movie at the nearby drive-in cinema. The Nitestar was situated on the Mutare road and was within walking distance from where we lived. The three of us were well skilled at deceiving our parents by telling them we would be staying at each other's houses and thereby freeing ourselves up for the night. It was early on a Saturday evening that we took the walk from the leafy suburb of Highlands to the drive-in and entered through a hole in the fence under the cover of darkness. The huge parking area was tarred and had rows of humps in the surface to enable cars to position themselves in order to get the best view of the giant outdoor screen. We positioned ourselves to the far left of the takeaway and bar in the centre and set up a sleeping bag on the slope near a speaker. We watched both the early and late shows and played on a small Nintendo Donkey Kong machine I had got from South Africa, during the film intervals. The three of us slept the night there and woke at the crack of dawn the next day. A discussion started about our respective fates and before long it was decided that we should run away from home. My reason was purely that I did not want to go to Plumtree while Buckley's reason was that he wanted to go to live in South Africa with his father. Mann's reason was simply to come along for the ride. We decided we would make our way to the border city of Mutare, cross into Mozambique, make our way to the port city of Beira where we would stow away on a cargo ship to England. At the time it sounded like a fine idea, so armed with nothing but a single sleeping bag and a hand-held video game, we made our way to the nearby railway tracks. The morning goods train came along soon enough and stopped at a nearby siding. We climbed into the guard carriage at the back and asked the guard if we could hitch a ride. He was a bit suspicious at first but after some persuasion he agreed that we could go along with him. The empty carriage had nothing at all inside it apart from some filthy old sacks and as the train departed, the carriage was filled with blowing, choking coal and tobacco dust.

The 80 km journey to the town of Marondera took a good three hours and it was decided on arrival that we needed a faster method of transport. We thanked the guard, dusted ourselves off, and headed to the main road to hitch a lift in a car. It didn't take long for a vehicle to stop and the three of us bundled into an old Peugeot driven by an elderly white man who was somewhat taken aback to find three young boys hitch hiking alone across the country. We gave the old man some excuses and told him we had been given permission by our parents, and that we were simply on our way to visit friends in Mutare. The old man had no choice but to accept our explanation and soon enough we were on our way to the border. We arrived in Mutare late that afternoon and after thanking the old man we said our goodbyes and headed off. The old man had become increasingly suspicious and worried for us during our journey, and we had no idea at the time that he actually reported us as suspected runaways to the Mutare police after dropping us off. One of the main landmarks in Mutare is the imposing Cross Kopje, a high rocky hill separated from the vast mountainous terrain of the Eastern border. Atop it is the 10 metre high granite cross built in 1924 in memory of black soldiers who died in East Africa in World War One. After a few conversations with some locals we learned that the invisible border with Mozambique lay just beyond it so we began making our way there. The official border post, Machipanda, lies roughly 5 km to the South and we knew full well that we should avoid it at all costs. The late afternoon was darkening towards early evening by the time we reached the foot of the rocky hill and began climbing. We reached the summit at dusk and far in the distance we saw the twinkling lights of the Mozambican town of Manica. Foolishly we began climbing down the back of the hill and making our way towards the distant lights but soon found ourselves in dark and impenetrable jungle.

We hunkered down for the night on an area of flat ground and attempted to sleep. It was some hours later that we heard voices nearby.

"Jesus," said Buckley. "I hope they're not dissidents."

Whoever it was that had been nearby soon passed and we were left with only the darkness and noises of the night.

We awoke at the crack of dawn to find we were in a thick forest surrounded by vines and massive trees. There was still a fair distance to travel down the slope towards the base of the hill so we began our journey into 'no man's land' immediately. On our way down we crossed a rusted old fence that had a red triangular sign on it. Buckley took the sign as a memento. On both sides were painted a skull and crossbones with the words 'Perigo Minas', Danger Mines. I will never know if we walked through a minefield, but we survived and emerged on the flatter lands beyond. We walked for an hour or two until we reached the railway line that ran into Mozambique. By then the thought of actually crossing into Mozambique was becoming a little frightening so we decided to set up camp near the railway line in 'no man's land'. We were hungry and thirsty, but we attempted to make a crude hut using tree branches and leaves. With no tools or experience this idea fell flat and we spent the rest of the day swimming and climbing rocks at a nearby river. By the time the sun was going down we were ravenously hungry. At the top of a nearby hill stood a lonely mud hut so we made our way up to see if we could find some food. It was nearly 6.00 pm when the owner returned from work in Mutare. The old man spoke no English but he welcomed us into his home and gave us a meal of sadza (maize meal) and stew which we ate by the light of a paraffin lamp. That night we slept on the hard mud floor of his hut and woke as he left for work the following morning. With nothing much to do we decided to make our way down the hill and to spend the day swimming in the river once again. It was mid-afternoon when hunger struck once again so we decided to jump a train into Mutare to find some food. With goods trains passing every few hours, it was easy enough to run alongside and jump on to the foot rails of the freight carriages. From there it was an easy ride into the city where we alighted before reaching the station. By then we were very dirty and having no other clothes we must have looked a sight walking into the city.

We chose a busy supermarket and emerged a few minutes later with tins of bully beef and bread rolls stuffed into our shorts. Mann could not help returning after we had eaten to lift three small tubs of ice cream for dessert. We ate like street urchins in the back alleys of the city and once full, we made our way back to the station to jump another train 'home'. That night the old man who had allowed us to sleep in his hut returned after dark and once again prepared a meal for us. I have no idea what he thought of three young white boys suddenly arriving out of nowhere and deciding to stay with him. Still, he was gracious and fed us, while saying very little. It was the next afternoon when the three of us got into an argument over the Donkey Kong machine. I can't remember what it was about but I stormed off and made my way into town in the late afternoon. There were no trains at that time of day so the walk was long and I only made it to the station when it was dark at around 7.00 pm. It was as I was walking towards the city centre that the two police officers saw me and arrested me. It was clear they knew who I was and they questioned me as to where my fellow runaways were. I refused to answer but was marched off to the charge office at the police station immediately. It must have been 8.00 pm by the time we arrived and I was told to sit on a wooden bench and stay put while the officers kept a beady eye on me. Eventually a young white lady constable arrived and took me aside to talk. Of course her main line of questioning was as to the whereabouts of my fellow runaways. Once again, I refused to talk and cheekily demanded food and cigarettes instead. I can clearly recall her frustration as she brought her face close to mine and scolded me angrily. Eventually she stormed off and returned soon after with a takeaway box of rice and stew, and ten Madison cigarettes.

That night I slept on the wooden bench of the charge office under the watch of the officers on duty, but it was the next morning when I was moved to the main police camp. By then our parents had been informed that one of us had been found and I knew that they were on their way to Mutare to collect us. I was taken to the rooms of the officer in charge of Manicaland. On the way there I was warned that he was a no-nonsense chap who would not allow any arrogance or cheek from me.

The huge man sat behind an expansive desk almost bursting out of his uniform. I took a seat in front of him and he regarded me with mild annoyance.

"You young boys have caused us a lot of trouble, " he said in his Shona accent. "Where are your friends?"

I knew that I was in a position of power so I decided to use my bargaining skills before telling them where Mann and Buckley were.

"I will say nothing until I get a packet of thirty Madison," I replied.

The big man bristled with anger and beads of sweat began to form on his temples. He shouted an instruction in Shona to a subordinate who scurried off to get my cigarettes. It was only when he returned that I sat back after lighting up and told them.

"They are in the area beyond Cross Kopje," I said. "No man's land."

Immediately the big man gave a set of instructions to his junior and a team of maybe twenty-five policemen were sent off to conduct a sweep of the area. They returned a couple of hours later with Mann and Buckley in tow. I guess for us the adventure was over and although we hadn't actually made it to Mozambique we had been on the adventure of a lifetime.

"You boys are filthy!" we were told by a lady constable. "You will now go for showers before your parents get here."

We were all led to an ablution block where we found soap and towels. Rebellious to the end we climbed up the water pipes and put muddy hand and footprints on the walls and ceilings of the place.

It was about an hour later that my father arrived in his car with Mann's step-dad. After they had had a few quiet words with the officer in charge we left Mutare and began the three-hour journey back to Harare. Very little was said on the way, but I remember there being a tin of Milo in the back of the car which we ate quietly on the way. We arrived at Buckley's house hours later and I remember him walking sheepishly towards his mother who stood with her hands on her hips in the doorway. As he walked in she clipped him across his ear and they disappeared inside the house. Mann and his step-dad were dropped off without any drama and I returned home with my father. To be honest I'm not sure what I expected when I returned home. No doubt we had put our parents through a tough time but there was no shouting or major punishment. Instead I was allowed to go quietly to my room and life continued as normal. But for us there was no change in plan. We were still going to Plumtree School in a few weeks' time.

CHAPTER THREE

The Plumtree Bus

It was early in the morning, the day before the school term was due to start, that we dressed in our number one uniforms with blazers, ties, and long trousers. Our trunks were loaded into my father's car and we left home to go to meet the Plumtree bus. Ahead of us was an eight-hour journey into the unknown and my brother and I were shitting ourselves, to put it mildly. We drove through the city in silence until we reached the car park of the Harare museum where the bus awaited. Painted green with a red stripe down the side and a white roof, it was a most frightening sight for my brother and I. Milling around were school kids of all ages, some scared looking new boys, and others wizened and knowing. Overall there was an atmosphere of quiet acceptance as the workers loaded the many black steel trunks on to the roof rack of the old bus. Eventually there was a roll call and we hugged our parents as we said goodbye and boarded the bus. Once fully loaded, the engine started and we drove off heading south down the Bulawayo road. My brother and I sat together talking to no-one as we went. The mood was solemn and bleak. What no-one knew, including my brother, was the fact that I had secretly packed a set of civilian clothes in the rucksack that sat near my feet. I also had a small amount of pocket money with me which I intended to use to carry out my second escape plan. I was quite determined that I would not go to Plumtree School. I broke the news to my brother about an hour into the journey. He accepted it with wide eyes but promised to keep quiet about it regardless. The bus stopped at the small town of Norton to pick up a few boys before continuing its journey. It was about an hour later that we pulled into the small hotel in the mining town of Kadoma. Here we were to pick up another load of boys before continuing to Kwekwe and Bulawayo. The morning was bright and hot as I climbed out of the bus with a few other boys who needed to use the toilet.

"Hurry up," we were told as we walked into the gloomy interior of the hotel.

Upon arriving in the toilets, I made a bee line for a cubicle rather than the urinal.

I locked the door as the rest of the boys finished their business, and quietly changed out of my uniform into my civvies. With my uniform packed in the rucksack I listened for any movement. There was none, and I slipped quietly out of the toilets and headed deeper into the hotel looking for an exit to the rear. I walked casually through the kitchens and emerged at a service area at the back of the building. From there I turned left and walked north trying to put as much distance between myself and where I knew the bus to be. It was as I reached the main road and hid in the shade of a Flamboyant tree that I saw the bus leaving. It trundled off down the main street, its driver and occupants completely oblivious to the fact that one of the boys was missing. I had done it again. It was a short walk through the town of Kadoma to the bus stop where I boarded a Harare bound rural bus. Although it was cramped and noisy, I was free and heading homewards. I had no real plan as to what I would do when I got back to Harare, but I was satisfied with the immense feeling of relief at having escaped. It was mid-afternoon by the time the bus arrived in Harare and I alighted near the show grounds in the south of town. I walked through the bustling heat of the city on Samora Machel Avenue until I reached Enterprise road. I can't remember exactly what prompted me to go to my Grandmother's flat which was nearby. It was probably thirst or hunger, but I went there regardless. She lived on the second floor of a small block in Eastlea. Of course, I had no intention of alerting her to my presence so instead I went to the gardener's room at the rear of the property. Initially he was welcoming as he knew me vaguely from previous visits and allowed me to sit in his room and drink some water. But I think it was when I told him not to tell my Grandmother that I was there that he smelled a rat. It was as I tried to leave that he grabbed me by the wrist with a grip like steel and locked me in his room. I was busted yet again. Unable to move I sat in the small room and awaited my fate. It arrived in the form of my father who had been telephoned by my Grandmother. With quiet calm, he led me to his car while my worried looking Grandmother stood watching from the balcony above.

The fact that I was missing from the school bus was only discovered upon arrival at Plumtree. No doubt phone calls were made and things kept quiet, but I'm sure there were consequences for those who were responsible. That night I remember my father making numerous phone calls while I sat in the lounge watching television. Once done, he walked in and made a calm announcement.

"Tomorrow we are flying to Bulawayo and then I will drive you to Plumtree," he said. "You will go to school!"

With that dreadful news I went to bed and awoke early the next day to get the morning flight to Bulawayo. My father hired a car at the airport and eventually we found our way to the Plumtree road. The countryside was completely different to that of Mashonaland in that it was arid with sparse thorny bush and sandy soils. My father did his best to reassure me on the way which actually made me feel a bit better about my situation. We arrived at the imposing school gates an hour later and drove to the administration block. I waited in the car while my father went to see the headmaster who directed us to

Milner House and Mr West, the housemaster. Knowing my background, I guess I was treated with kid gloves initially, and was led to my dormitory and shown my bed and locker in the company of my father. My initial impressions were that it was not as bad as I had expected.

The buildings were old and full of history, the grounds were green and pleasant, and there was an air of calm to the place. Being mid-morning, all of the boys were in classes at the time, and I took a walk around the house with Mr West and my father. Eventually, and I'm sure with great relief, my father said goodbye and drove back to Bulawayo to get his return flight. It was then, after much argument and reluctance, after fighting tooth and nail, that I finally found myself at Plumtree School.

CHAPTER FOUR

The First Days

I guess it wasn't as bad as I had expected. The boys from Milner house returned at lunch time and I was introduced to those in my dormitory before following them to the dining hall for lunch. There were of course questions from the boys about my leaving the bus the previous day and what I had done afterwards. They seemed fascinated by this brazen act of rebellion and this put me in a somewhat elevated position at first. The walk to the 'graze hall' took us past the swimming pool with its view of the back of Lloyd House, the headmaster's house in a lush garden to the right, and finally Gaul House in the distance. The boys filed silently into the hall in orderly fashion and queued patiently at the row of bain-maries to be served their food on prison style metal trays. Once loaded with lunch, dessert, and a blue plastic mug of juice, we made our way to our assigned bench tables and sat down. At the top of each table was a senior known as the 'head of table'. In my case it was a particularly tough looking boy by the name of Garrard. Immediately I decided it would be prudent to not make any eye contact with him and get on with lunch instead.

"Not yet," whispered the boy seated next to me. "Wait."

It turned out that no one was allowed to eat until a grace had been said. Eventually everyone was seated and one of the white-shirt-wearing prefects at the top table stood up and spoke.

"For these and all his many mercies may The Lord make us truly thankful," he said.

"Amen," said every single boy in the hall in reply.

With that there was a deafening clatter of cutlery on metal trays and a sudden outburst of loud conversation amongst the boys.

The food, as I soon learned, was terrible. During my time at the school a number of foreign objects such as bullets, twigs, leaves, nails, and hair were found in our meals. We came to accept this as a novelty of sorts. After lunch the boys took a slow walk back to the house for the daily rest period. This was for forty-five minutes on our beds during which there was the option of either sleep or conversation. My first rest period was spent answering questions about my escape from the bus. In similar fashion to the dining room, in each dormitory there was a senior boy, ostensibly to maintain order. I learned then that one could only address a senior if the words 'Excuse me' were said before each and every sentence. This was abbreviated to 'Sme' but it was expected and indeed demanded as part of the school's strict seniority rules. It was also ruled that no boy should *ever* address a senior unless spoken to. I soon learned that the entire school operated on a complex and age-old system of seniority and privileges that had been in place since the beginning. So intricate was this largely unspoken system that upon reaching the 4th form, boys would automatically earn no less than 120 privileges. These would range from the seemingly ridiculous and unimportant to the most revered such as the privilege of wearing Veldskoen bush shoes as opposed to the standard school footwear. The rest period was followed by afternoon prep. The junior boys all filed into the prep room for an hour of silence and study. Any boy caught talking or passing notes during prep was instantly given an imposition, otherwise known as an impot. This punishment was an hour of manual labour to be carried out on Saturday mornings. Some boys would receive up to 5 or 6 impots in a week effectively ruining the precious free time afforded them on weekends. The time after prep was usually reserved for sport, although it being the beginning of term, I found I had a free hour or so which I used to visit my young brother in the first form Hammond House. All boys had to report back to their houses for shower time at around 4.30 pm after which there would be a parade and a military style roll call. The names were read out in alphabetical order and each boy was required to respond by saying the word 'adsum' abbreviated to 'sum' meaning 'present' in Latin. After this was the trek to the dining hall for dinner with all the same routines as any other meal.

Dinner would be followed by 2 hours of prep during which there was absolute silence once again. For me this was a mind-numbing experience and I found myself reading a lot of books to stifle the boredom. Prep was quickly followed by bed and lights out. To be honest I think it was a shock to my system and I found it difficult to accept that there was very little free time at all. I did, however, discover the boiler room at the back of the house. Filthy dirty and full of coal, it was hardly visited by the boys, and proved to be a very easy place to visit during the day and night to have a cigarette. This was the first of many secret places I would discover during my time at the school. So all in all, it was not a very happy time for me. I liked the old buildings and the history of the place, but I felt like an outsider of sorts. Time seemed to drag on endlessly and friends were few. In my mind I wondered how long I could take it.

CHAPTER FIVE

The First Few Weeks

It wasn't long before I started to gauge the various personalities in the dormitory and the house as a whole. There was a mixture of sporty jock types and the more nerdy academic type boys. I'm not sure where I fitted in if at all as I was neither. I knew full well that staying away from and avoiding eye contact with seniors, would serve me well, as to me they looked like grown men. Many of them had beard stubble and would have to shave from time to time. Some were mostly fair and relatively friendly but many were known as being cruel and potentially violent to those juniors they disliked. Some afternoons I would take a walk with an equally outcast or alienated boy across Patterson Field in front of the grand Beit Hall. To the right of the field was the cricket pavilion and beyond it the hockey pitch and boundary fence. I soon found that the pavilion was a good spot to smoke in the afternoons and I found myself going there for that reason almost daily. Another building of interest was the armoury. Positioned to the left of Grey House on the edge of Patterson field, it was a heavily secured building with bolted steel doors and thick bars in its small dirty windows. On one occasion I placed two bricks beneath a window, stood on them and peered inside. It came as no surprise, after rubbing away the dust, to see the rows of rifles and other firearms within. The school, after all, was extremely remote and located on the border with Botswana. There had been a lot of activity in the area during the bush war and this was still evident everywhere with the high security fence and grenade screens on the house widows etc. It was common knowledge that during the war, all teachers and prefects were armed 24/7 with Uzi sub-machine guns. To me it appeared the building was impenetrable. It turned out later that it was not. The Saturday night movie was a welcome respite from the boredom and routine. The entire school would dress in their number ones (long trousers, ties and blazers) and congregate in the Beit Hall for some escapism thanks to the film club who were responsible for maintaining the projector and running the film on the big screen.

On one occasion the school was 'treated' to the movie 'Woodstock'. I clearly remember most of the boys being bored or confused by the hippie music and antics but I, for one, was captivated by the electric performances by The Who and Jimi Hendrix. There were a number of other clubs and societies one could join. The falconry club was of interest as the boys kept live birds of prey and would regularly hunt with them as well as looking after the birds. One boy from Grey house, Smilie, had a fully grown owl which he kept in a shed at the back of the house. Sadly, it died one day after being fed pickled beetroot. The fact that I was a secret smoker soon became known by the seniors in the house. This was a bugbear for the sportier type seniors and prefects who were non-smokers. On one occasion I was berated on the school running track by a particularly nasty prefect from Hwange by the name of Williams.

"Run you nicotine stained little prick!" he shouted with genuine malice from the sidelines as I battled along the cinder surface.

Suffice to say, I was not a fan of Williams, but I did like his other brothers, Spike and Bloat. But for the seniors who were smokers I represented someone who could be used. Soon enough I was approached by one of them who asked me to go to the village to buy cigarettes for him. With no real way to say no, I found myself dressing in my number ones, applying for a village pass, and making my way into the tiny railway town to find a general dealer who would sell me a few boxes of Madison cigarettes. I returned from the trip without being discovered and delivered the contraband to the senior in question. He was very pleased and soon after I found myself being recruited as a cigarette mule on a regular basis. This new business put me in good stead with some but at the same time it made me the focus of attention of other senior boys I had hoped to avoid. They knew I was up to something and they made it their mission to find out what it was.

One weekend it was decided that there would be a clay larkie battle at Gaul dam. This dam was situated just beyond the boundary fence and was visible from the upper floors of Gaul House. As the dam was located outside the school grounds, the entire house had arranged bush exits (a weekend day bush pass) and after breakfast and church we all left the school and made our way along the railway lines to the venue. The dam itself was shallow and surrounded by sticky black clay. With the seniors on one side we all proceeded to collect and store our ammunition which consisted of huge lumps of clay. A number of boys waded out into the water to collect clay and they came back with blood sucking leeches attached to their legs. Our weapons were long flexible sticks we had ripped from nearby trees. A lump of clay was moulded into a ball and attached to the thinner end of said stick. Once whipped in the direction of the enemy the lumps of clay would be flicked off the sticks at astonishing speed. Soon enough a full-blown war ensued across the dam with hundreds of missiles flying at any given time. At one stage I was hit in the middle of my back and the impact threw me to the ground winded and left a dark purple welt on my skin. The afternoon ended with the exhausted boys making their way back to the school for showers and dinner after the usual roll call. I guess that night as I lay in my bed, I decided that Plumtree School wasn't all that bad. It had been a fun weekend and I was starting to make some friends. There were, of course, some seniors and other boys who had knives out for me, but I was gaining ground and finding my feet. I was learning how to manipulate the system and figuring out how to make it work for me.

CHAPTER SIX

Teachers & Army Games

There were a number of interesting characters who were teachers at the school at the time. The eccentric Milner housemaster Harold West was one of them. The highly intelligent, well-spoken old Englishman had a good sense of humour but he displayed some very strange behaviour when he became annoyed or angry. It would usually begin with his bushy grey eyebrows twitching and then soon after he would start rubbing and clapping his hands together and gently slapping them on his sides. This would become more intense the angrier he became and his voice would grow in volume. It was a comical sight, but the boys knew to keep quiet when it happened as it could quite easily explode into a full-blown tantrum.

"Muck!" he would shout in his posh accent. "You're nothing but muck boy!"

Then there was the sneaky and secretive housemaster of Lloyd House, Jub Jub. I cannot recall his real name but he was known for his cunning and ingenuity in exposing any wrong doing by the boys. Another teacher was a dreadful old drunk by the name of Mr 'Wax' Candler. His other job was that of being the pastor of the church. A lot of boys were convinced he was still inebriated from the teacher's bar (Peddar Bar) while giving his sermons in church on Sunday mornings. He lived in a tiny cottage near what became the computer room and was often seen stumbling around drunk in the evenings. His swollen nose was purple and engorged by alcohol. One of the favourite teachers at the time was a red-haired young man by the name of Laurie Allen. His subject was history and he would often spend an entire lesson relating a certain event from the past in an interesting and interactive way with the boys. His novel teaching method was engaging for us and we would look forward to his lessons as they were fascinating and didn't really feel like school at all. Then there was our maths teacher, Mr 'Cane Rat' Shadwell. Given his nickname for his buck teeth, he was an affable and chatty fellow, if a little goofy.

His favourite movie was The Mechanic starring Charles Bronson. On one occasion I recall him bowling a cricket ball at full speed in class down the line of desks. The heavy ball hit and injured a friend of mine, Spek, at the back of the class, much to his dismay. One of the few female teachers was a highly strung and very nervous lady by the name of Mrs 'Ma' Murgatroyd. Her subject was geography and I can recall the boys needling and questioning her repeatedly until she would physically shake and spin the end of her faux-gold chain belt on her waist in frustration. I'm sure she was a bit of a boozer as well. I cannot forget the deputy housemaster of Milner house, Mr 'Pin Jaw' Hogbin. Another strange man, he would wander the corridors and prep room whistling to himself loudly. He wore huge 1970's style glasses and had an extremely wide jawline, hence his name. He was known for using his huge glasses to literally see behind him. I remember one night in prep a boy from my form, Heath, was silently gesticulating behind him. Pin Jaw spun around suddenly and clapped him across the head.

"You had no idea," he said triumphantly. "With these glasses I can see behind me!"

He was also known for his strong conviction that boys below the fourth year should not be allowed to exist. I guess he saw us as an annoyance. One of the more memorable teachers was a tall gangly Mauritian man with long fingernails by the name of Mr Ramtoola. With long untidy black hair and thick, square 1970's style glasses, he was known as 'Space Monkey'. He too was not immune to the needling of the boys and on one occasion I had annoyed him so much he called me up to stand near him at the blackboard. I cannot recall the question, but my answer enraged him enough to strike at me with his right hand. Fortunately, I ducked in time and he broke several of his fingernails on the blackboard behind me. I'm not sure how long he lasted at the school, but I do know his time there was far from pleasant. One particularly nasty teacher was the Grey House master by the name of Mr 'Bop' Thomson.

A tall, fat, old and angry man, he was known for giving boys who were having issues with each other sets of boxing gloves and encouraging them to fight on the lawn in front of Grey House. I found out much later after leaving school, that there were stories of him having sexually abused boys at Plumtree some 20 years previously, and the story had been subsequently covered up. It was said he had been slapped on the wrist by the authorities and sent to teach in South Africa until returning to Zimbabwe much later to teach once again. I have no idea if this was true but I do know that this sort of thing was prevalent and common in schools in Zimbabwe at the time. No one can deny this. One of the more colourful characters was the woodwork teacher who went by the name of Mr 'Don' Mudge. A veteran of the second world war, he was clearly extremely shell shocked and suffered from PTSD. The story was that he had been in a tank when it had been blown up on the battlefield and had spent several days trapped inside said tank with a dead compatriot while awaiting rescue. A harmless and cheerful old man, he would constantly mutter to himself and was never far from his constant companion, Nipper, a small Jack Russell dog. One boy in my dormitory, Ross Darlow, was particularly good at woodwork. A tall, cheerful chap with blonde hair, he came from a huge ranch in the West Nicholson area of Zimbabwe. His father would fly into the school in his light aircraft to pick him up at exeat weekends and school holidays. Darlow was very proficient at fashioning realistic looking replica pistols and rifles from scraps of wood and pieces of steel piping. His skills were such that his work was in great demand and he spent most afternoons in the woodwork shop making these weapons. Every boy in my dormitory ordered a gun from Darlow and paid him with a few cents of pocket money for the job. It was decided one week that there would be army games in the bush that Sunday. The dormitory was split into two squads that would either patrol or lie in ambush for the others prior to an attack. The bush exits were booked and early on the following Sunday morning after church we trekked out towards Tegwani and into the thick bush to start our war games. The boys hid behind anthills, inside clumps of thorn bush and up trees to lie in wait for the 'enemy' to pass.

The battles only stopped at lunch time when a truce was called and we all sat together to eat the disgusting dry hamburgers which had been given to us by the staff at the graze hall. After a short rest, and with some mild indigestion, the army games continued until much later when it was time to return to the school. Filthy dirty, we all made our way back to Milner House for showers, roll call, dinner, prep, and bed. It had been another good weekend and I had managed to stay out of trouble. At least for then.

CHAPTER SEVEN

Nicknames & Secret Spots

One thing that struck me on arrival at Plumtree School was the number of strange and amusing nicknames. Not only reserved for the teachers, there were plenty assigned to the boys as well. More often than not, they were reflective of certain physical aspects or behaviours of the boys. For instance, before I arrived at the school I had been given a small telescope by my grandmother. On occasions I would stand at one of the windows of my second-floor dormitory and look out at the school through it. This resulted in me being given the temporary nickname of Galileo until it was decided that I would be known as Wally. One boy was simply known as Suitcase because instead of carrying his books in the common green canvas rucksacks, he used, well, a suitcase. Another red-haired boy who was tall and quite portly was known as Obelix from the well-known Asterix comics. But there were many others such as Bodger, Tomato, Bloat, Beechie, Stumps, Spike, Kuks, Archie, Steel, Spaz, Burt, Macko, Spek, Rosy, and countless others. With time I gradually became more integrated with the boys of Milner House and others in my form from the rest of the houses. It is said that birds of a feather flock together and this was very true when it came to

Plumtree School. There were a number of boys in my form from other houses who smoked cigarettes and when there was free time we would inevitably meet. A lot of these boys had been at the school since their first year and as a result they knew all of the best places in which to disappear for a spell. One of the more memorable was under the Afrikaans class in the school quadrangle near the Beit Hall. It must have taken generations of boys to patiently dig it out but when the desks in the class were moved and the old wooden trapdoor in the floor lifted, we could climb down and enter a subterranean world of darkness and seclusion. At least 20 cubic metres of soil had been painstakingly removed over the years and carried to some unknown location. What was left was a hollowed-out earth bunker of sorts, furnished with school chairs and tables.

Lighting was either from the air vents at the side of the base of the building or from candles that were placed around the seating area. A cool and dark place, we spent many hours smoking, chatting, and later drinking down there, completely unseen by anyone. Then there was the attic above the Beit Hall. A massive expansive space filled with wooden beams, we would climb up there from the backstage area of the hall and be certain that no one would know we were there. One day we were making our way back down the ladders when Felix West arrived below to give a piano lesson to one of the music students. I recall spending a full hour clinging to the ladder silently as we waited for the lesson to end. Another notable occurrence up there, which I know to be true, was when one of my fellow smokers (name withheld) caught another boy masturbating on the deserted stage below. I was personally not there but the poor boy was confronted and forced up into the attic where he was repeatedly humiliated and had the end of his penis burnt with a lighter. I can only imagine that he was damaged for life, but this sort of extreme brutality was accepted if not commonplace. I recall one boy in Milner House who had been born with a third nipple. He hated it and was teased often about it. He removed it one afternoon with a set of nail clippers. Needless to say there was a lot of blood and laughter followed by a trip to the school hospital to see the matron Mrs 'Ma' Meaden. The boiler at Lloyd house was another favourite spot for an afternoon smoke. We would have to climb up an ancient steel ladder to a platform near the chimney, and although it was hot and dirty, we would be free to smoke. There were normally three tiny bats hanging upside down sleeping on a wooden beam nearby. They would sneeze comically in their slumber when we blew smoke at them. Of course, any opportunity for a village or bush exit was a virtual ticket to freedom. There was a small general dealer's shop on the dusty Tegwani Road where I would buy cigarettes and the owners would allow us to sit in the yard around the back of the shop. Those first weeks actually got better and better for me although the time dragged terribly. My only goal was to make it to the exeat weekend where we would all go home for a few days before returning to complete the term.

The only contact with our parents was to write and receive letters which we often did. In emergencies there was the option of making a reversed charges phone call from the old wind up telephone near the tuck shop, although we rarely did this. Instead we were left with grinding routine of school life for what seemed an eternity.

CHAPTER EIGHT

The Dudley Walton Outing.

One mysterious resident of Plumtree village was an old white man by the name of Dudley Walton. Very little was known of him apart from the fact that he lived in an old farmhouse in the bush on the Tegwani Road. He would regularly arrive at school rugby matches in a beaten up old short-wheelbase Land Rover with some other bearded men and sit in the back of the vehicle to watch the match from the sidelines. He never spoke to any of the boys, so he remained a bit of an enigma to most. During one such rugby match I was sitting next to a fellow smoker from Grey House by the name of Smilie. I asked if he knew anything about the man and he told me that Dudley Walton was a notorious drinker. He was known for his love of Mainstay Cane spirit and would crush the top of each bottle underfoot each time he opened one to indicate he would not stop drinking until it was finished. Smilie also told me that he would gladly allow boys from the school to join him in these drinking sessions. An idea was formed in our minds and one weekday afternoon Smilie and I made our way into the village to find some alcohol. We returned to the school later with a quarter bottle of cane and began planning our visit to Dudley Walton's house. We decided that the best night to visit would be a Friday as that was and remains, a party night in Zimbabwe. Our plan was to meet up an hour after lights out, sneak out of the school grounds, and make our way to his house where we would introduce ourselves and hopefully have a bit of a session. So the following Friday night I lay awake in my bed keeping an eye on the time and waiting for the dormitory to fall asleep. Ten minutes before our scheduled meeting time I climbed out of bed and quietly slipped out of the house. There was a full moon that night but I was wearing my dark green school tracksuit so I was fairly well camouflaged. I made my way out of the house grounds past the giant Marula tree at the front and then walked past the armoury on to Patterson field. I stood under the eaves of the cricket pavilion and waited for Smilie to arrive from Grey House.

The time passed slowly and at one stage I thought he might have been apprehended trying to leave Grey House and that I should give up on the mission and return to Milner. Then suddenly there was the thudding sound of footfalls on the field and the tracksuit clad figure of Smilie sprinting towards me materialised out of the darkness.

"I thought you weren't coming," I whispered.

"Sorry I'm late," he panted in reply. "Let's go."

We set off across the hockey field and climbed the tall security fence at the boundary of the school. From there it was a short walk through the bush to the Tegwani Road where we made a right turn and headed out of the village. I think it may have been about 2km to the rusted signpost that marked the dirt road to the house of Dudley Walton. Hearing music from inside we approached silently from the rear and crept up to the lounge window. What we saw came as a huge shock and filled us both with panic. Passed out drunk on the couch in the lounge was none other than our history teacher, the popular Laurie Allen. He had clearly gone there with the same intention as us. Smilie and I immediately retreated into the darkness to re-think our situation. We knew that if he were to wake and see us, we would be in serious trouble. Extreme caution was needed. Eventually Dudley Walton stumbled into the kitchen to refill a water jug and we whispered to him from our hiding place. The old man came out and greeted us with blood shot eyes and genuine surprise. We explained our predicament to which he agreed to supply us with some orange cordial and two glasses with which we could drink our booze but on the condition that we were not to set foot in the old farmhouse. We agreed and spent the next hour listening to the music and drinking near the kennels at the back of the house. When we were done we thanked Mr Walton and headed back up the road to the school. We climbed the fence at the same spot we had exited and said goodbye before making our way back to our respective houses. It had been a nerve racking but exciting nocturnal outing, and it would not be the last.

CHAPTER NINE

Spike Arrives

At the time that I had arrived at the school the headmaster was a man by the name of J.B. Clark. A quiet studious man nearing the end of his career, he was rarely seen on the school grounds and he left at the end of my first term. The school was awash with rumours of who would be the next headmaster – the most likely was thought to be the current head of Ellis Robbins High School in Harare. A man by the name of Mr Wilson. Not a lot was known about this person apart from the fact he had a fearsome reputation as an extremely strict educator and that he was a man of few words who both believed in and meted out severe punishment for any wrongdoings. This was confirmed beyond any doubt when he arrived at the school along with a hundred or so new boys from Ellis Robbins, 'Fush', the following term. The atmosphere of the school changed markedly and it was suddenly as if things were shaken up and would never be the same again. The news that there would be an address from the new headmaster the following day in the school chapel spread like wildfire through the classes and dormitories and we all waited with baited breath in anticipation of this event. It was with a distinct sense of foreboding that the entire school filed silently into the chapel early the following morning to await the address from the as-yet unseen Mr Wilson. As if to create a sense of drama and anticipation we were made to sit in silence for a further ten minutes, the only sound being that of the occasional church pew scraping on the stone floor or a boy clearing his throat. The man's arrival, when it finally came, was as dramatic a scene as I have ever witnessed. Wearing a long flowing black gown and a traditional mortar board (an academic cap with a stiff, black, square top and a tassel) the tall thin man strode into the building from a side door and took his place behind a pulpit at the front. Without looking at the boys he placed his papers on the pulpit and began paging through them slowly. The entire school sat watching, completely spellbound as they waited. When he finally looked up and spoke it was with the deep booming voice of a man of wisdom, authority, and one who made it clear from the very start, that things were about to change forever. There were no formal introductions or genial greetings from the man.

Instead he glared at us all with his cold blue eyes and eventually he spoke.

"From now on all boys will do this.... " he began.

"From now on all boys will be subject to this....." he continued.

"From now on no boys will be allowed to do this...." he went on.

"All boys will be required to do the following...." he boomed.

This blunt and harsh monologue continued for a good five minutes until he finally folded and pocketed his papers and placed both hands on the pulpit.

"That is the message!" were his final words before he turned and walked out of the chapel with his long black gown billowing behind him.

The entire school was left in a state of shock as they absorbed what had just happened. When it came time to leave the chapel, we were all subjected to a spot haircut check and any boys found to have hair even a millimetre longer than the strict rules dictated were immediately given a double 'impot' and told to go directly for a haircut before school that very morning. The arrival of 'Spike' Wilson had shaken the foundations of the school and we knew things would never be the same. Later that year 'Spike' Wilson bought a dilapidated old ox wagon from someone in Bulawayo., He had the huge thing, originally from the days of the pioneer treks, transported to the school and set about the mammoth task of restoring it, with some seniors who were adept at woodwork. I recall months later, one Saturday morning, taking a ride on the back of it as he triumphantly sat on the front bench and drove the harnessed cattle and the freshly restored wagon through the school.

Although he was a fearsome character I respected 'Spike' and did my best to stay out of his way (not for long). It is very sad that in later years there were allegations of inappropriate sexual advances on certain boys, but like I said earlier in this book, sadly this was fairly commonplace in Zimbabwean boarding schools. Anyway, moving on.

CHAPTER TEN

The Tegwani Session

One of the more popular spots for a Sunday bush exit was the Tegwani rocks near Prison Dam. Situated about 10 km down the Tegwani Road we would often take the long walk there and spend the day exploring, climbing the rocks, and swimming in the shallow waters of the dam. Although filled with a powdery light grey clay, the water was free of leeches and weeds so we preferred swimming there to Gaul Dam near the school. One of the boys had a portable tape deck, although it was not allowed as it was a 5th year privilege, and we would sit on the rocks and listen to the South African band Evoid and their hit song 'Shadows' which was about the African Lion. It was decided one day that we should return to Tegwani rocks but this time to have a party with some alcohol. So the following Sunday found a group of about six of us from various houses, with a combined pot of pocket money, heading out into the bush. Sadly, for some reason I cannot recall, we were unable to buy any booze in Plumtree but we took the long walk regardless. We arrived at a local village of mud huts near the Tegwani rocks and began making polite enquiries about the availability of alcohol. An elderly man led us to a brew hut where he was in the process of making a batch of the illicit local opaque beer known as 'Seven day brew'. Our eyes lit up when we saw the 200 litre drum full of the stuff bubbling and fermenting away in the dark interior of the hut. A deal was struck and we left carrying around 30 litres of the grainy, pungent brew wired to a thick wooden pole in a disused plastic fertiliser sack. It was at a shady spot near the rocks that we sat down to drink and we passed a plastic mug around until it was finished. It was not long before we began to feel the effects of the alcohol and we all ran down to the dam for a swim. By the time we made it back to the rocks we were paralytically drunk and spent the next few hours rolling around in the dirt laughing uncontrollably. None of us could recall the long walk back to the school but on arrival we all made our way to our respective houses to pass out. With shower time and roll call imminent, many of us failed to make it and our friends covered for us by answering when our names were called.

One boy did make it down and he was held in a standing position by his dorm mates on either side. What we didn't know was that the alcohol we had consumed had only been brewing for 5 days when it was supposed to have done so for seven. Hence the name 'Seven day brew'. As a result of this the beer was too 'fresh' and it was about to have a common and terrible effect on us all. Having missed dinner I awoke at around 10.00 pm with a deep aching in my stomach along with appalling heartburn and a pounding headache. Before I could move I vomited violently in my bed. The strain of doing so also caused an uncontrollable bout of watery diarrhoea. Groaning miserably, I crawled on all fours to the toilets where I spent the next three hours repeating this process. The scene was nothing short of horrific. It was at around 6.00 am the next day when I finally showered and walked gingerly down to the school hospital to seek medical attention. I was greeted by the Plumtree nurse Mrs 'Ma' Meaden who nodded knowingly as I told her of my woes. She pointed me in the direction of the ward and told me to go to bed immediately. It was only as I pushed the double doors of the ward open that I was surprised to see my five other drinking buddies all laid up in beds along the length of the ward.

"Howzit Wally!" they said in unison. "What took you so long?"

The six of us spent the next three days happily convalescing at the school hospital, eating good food and reading old National Geographic magazines from the 1940's and 50's.

CHAPTER ELEVEN

The Bulawayo Trip

It must have been some time during my second year at the school that, as fourth year students we had acquired many privileges that we made sure of enjoying to the full. We were finally entitled to wear the coveted Veldskoen shoes after school, which to us was real progress. Some of the 'A' stream students even had their own studies that we would visit as much as possible. We were even allowed to make coffee in the evenings after prep. It was some time during that year that we got to hear of the big rugby match that was to be held at the Hartsfield Rugby Grounds in Bulawayo. I cannot remember who was playing but the match coincided with a fixture for the 2nd team water polo team in the same city. A lot of the boys in this team were known to us and we soon learned that they would be staying at the Bulawayo Holiday Inn for the night. We had all heard of the notorious bar at Hartsfield Rugby Grounds and we knew full well that there would be a huge party there on the day. A small group of us decided that we should attend at all costs as there would be much merriment and also the possibility of seeing some girls. To us it was an opportunity that could not be missed but the actual execution would need very careful and thorough planning. We were, after all, virtual prisoners in what was effectively a military academy in the middle of the bush. After a number of meetings it was decided that there would be an elaborate set of forged letters sent to our respective house masters informing them that we had been given permission to travel to Bulawayo on the train for the night and that we would be returning the following day. The letters said that our accommodation was taken care of as was our transport to and from the station. Our plan, of course, was to sneak into The Holiday Inn to join our friends, enjoy the free room service, and sleep the night. These letters, purportedly from our parents, were carefully crafted and then hand-written by a boy with immaculate handwriting (for a small fee) and individually posted to the school. Given that they were only travelling less than a few hundred metres they arrived within a few days and we were summoned by our house masters to inform us our parents' requests had been received and that permission for us to take a night's leave from the school was granted.

So it was early on a Saturday morning when we packed our rucksacks, dressed in our longs, blazers and ties, and armed with our gate passes we left the school and headed to the dusty Plumtree railway station. With great excitement we boarded the early train for the four-hour journey through the bush to Bulawayo. Due to our limited budget we were only able to afford 4th class tickets but we didn't mind a bit. We had changed into civilian clothes by the time we arrived at the sprawling historic station at around midday and began the long walk to the Hartsfield Rugby Grounds. By the time we arrived at around 2.00 pm there was a large crowd gathered on the grandstands and in the car park. The atmosphere was electric and we wandered through the hordes of party goers wide eyed and full of awe. Sadly our concerted efforts to get into the bar were thwarted but we did manage to get some beer which we took to the grandstands to drink as we watched the match. We left as it was getting dark and began walking back to the city to join our friends at the Holiday Inn. We arrived at the modern hotel at around 7.00 pm and after a grilling by the extremely suspicious staff we finally made it to our friends' rooms. Our efforts to get free drinks from room service came to naught however and it was not long before the manager arrived to check up on us. Sensing it was probably time to leave, we had one of the boys make a phone call to a local Bulawayo boy by the name of Bosman to ask if we could stay at his house. It turned out that he was an extremely friendly and welcoming character who lived in the suburbs with his single mother. She immediately drove into town to pick us up and we spent a pleasant night at their house eating, drinking beer, and listening to music. We were dropped at the railway station the following morning and caught the slow train back to Plumtree arriving in the late afternoon. Our secret excursion to Bulawayo had been a great success.

CHAPTER TWELVE

Problems with Sport

One thing that was very prominent and important to Plumtree School was sport. The school had a great reputation for this, especially in rugby, where the two titans of Matabeleland, Falcon College and Plumtree school, fought a constant battle for dominance. But there was also hockey, water polo, athletics, basketball, and cricket. Sport was a source of pride for the school and it took up most afternoons in one way or another. I had played rugby and cricket at my previous schools but never with much success. I simply wasn't very good at sports. So it was with guarded scepticism that I viewed the strong sporting culture of my new school. Being Matabeleland, the sports fields were dry and sandy in comparison to the lush soft green grass of the Mashonaland schools. From the beginning I did my very best to avoid all but essential or compulsory sporting activities. During the rugby season I told my seniors that I had chosen to play hockey. I then informed those in charge of hockey that I was playing rugby. On those particular afternoons I would slip away quietly to one of our secret spots and lie low for the duration, usually with friends from other houses. There were, however, a few activities that were near impossible to avoid. Athletics and cross country.

The school had a superb cinder running track near Gaul House and we would regularly find ourselves there for hours on end, training and running circuits. I dreaded those afternoons and I really battled with the 400m and 800m runs. A lot of the seniors, especially the sporty types, were aware that I was a smoker and they made their distaste of this fact clear as I wheezed and puffed around the track. Another activity that was near impossible to get out of was cross country. The entire house would congregate on the front lawns of Milner and the gruelling 10km run would begin. We would make our way past the chapel, out of the main gate, and run through the bush around the entire school near the boundary fence. The pace was fast and walking was forbidden making it especially gruelling in the heat and the dust of the afternoons.

On one occasion I managed to get out of cross country and a friend of mine and I climbed a tree near the chapel and sat there smoking, camouflaged in the branches, completely unseen as the entire house ran past sweating and panting below us. But for me there was one sporting activity that I really detested. Swimming. There was of course the well-known and much loved 'GP' (General Plunge) which could be announced at any time, even in the evenings after prep. On the rare occasions this happened, the entire house would hurriedly change into their swimming costumes, run down to the pool past the rising bell and leap into the water for a 10 minute unregulated swim. But Milner House had a particularly strong swimming regime and on the one occasion that I actually attended swimming training I really battled. The prefect in charge of swimming was a member of the first team water polo team and his training routine was especially punishing. He also had a distinct dislike of me and had singled me out on many occasions. I needed to devise a strategy that would see me excluded permanently from this activity, so I set about making enquiries from my friends from the other houses. It turned out that one of the juniors from Lloyd House had been suffering from earache and had visited the hospital the previous week. He had been given a letter by the matron excusing him from all swimming until he had been given the all clear. An idea formed in my mind and I set about composing a letter to that effect. Once I had finished the letter I had it re-written by a boy with neat handwriting and prepared myself for the con job. It was on a steaming hot afternoon I walked up to Williams with a plug of cotton wool stuffed in my ear. The letter, purportedly from the matron Mrs 'Ma' Meaden stated that I had a white fungus growing on my left ear drum and that I was to be strictly excluded from swimming until such time as it had cleared up. A deep frown formed on Williams' forehead as he read the note and his expression soon turned to one of utter disgust.

"Go away, Wallis," he said quietly as he handed the note back to me.

I walked away feeling very pleased with myself. My plan had worked and for the rest of the season I would not be expected anywhere near the swimming pool.

CHAPTER THIRTEEN

Music

One thing that played a big part in our lives at Plumtree School was music. Although it was strictly forbidden for any boy below 5th year to own any music reproduction device, some of us in the 4th year had portable tape decks which we would keep hidden away in case of random dorm inspections. I was the proud owner of a brand new and revolutionary device called a Walkman and I would listen to various compilation tapes in bed after lights out. There was a thriving underground tape exchange between friends in the various houses and as I said earlier in this book we would often listen to music while out on bush exits. I can't remember exactly who it was but one day a friend from Grey House approached me with a conspiratorial look on his face and pulled me aside.

"Wally," he said in hushed tones. "I've got some devil music. Heavy metal. Have you heard it?"

"No," I replied.

He pulled a nondescript tape from his pocket and handed it to me.

"Okay," he said. "Well, listen to this"

I asked my friend if he knew what bands they were but all he knew was that it was 'devil music'. Feeling puzzled and intrigued I thanked him, pocketed the tape, and got on with my day. I had no idea that there were two albums on that tape that would change my life forever. On the A side was 'The Number Of The Beast' by Iron Maiden while on the B side was 'Back In Black' by AC/DC. I had never heard of either band, but I remember looking forward to lights out that night to give it a listen.

So it was in bed later that night, in the darkness and silence when everyone was drifting off to sleep, that I put the headphones on and pressed play on my Walkman.

There was a long silence followed by the chilling spoken word intro to the album, 'The Number Of The Beast'.

"Woe to you o earth and sea, for the Devil sends the Beast with wrath, because he knows the time is short. Let him who hath understanding reckon the number of the Beast. For it is a human number. Its number is six hundred and sixty-six."

The words sent shivers down my spine and were quickly followed by what was and remains, a masterpiece of heavy music. The pounding, galloping drums, powerful soaring vocals, and blistering guitars conjured up visions of hell and warfare and mayhem, and I was instantly carried away to another world. As with all good music, it took me a few nights of listening to actually understand the complexities and intricacies of the album, but it grew on me, and surprised me every single time I heard it. I began looking forward to lights out every night when I would be free to listen to the album again and again. It was probably a week later when I finally listened to the album on the other side of the tape. 'Back In Black' by AC/DC was, and remains, a stone cold classic of rock music, and while not exactly metal, it was heavy and there were enough references to the Devil and Hell for it to sound equally evil and menacing. I loved both albums and still do to this day, but I was intrigued at how different they sounded while still being so heavy. I asked the friend who had given me the tape to explain the difference between the two bands. He told me that AC/DC was Country and Western heavy metal while the Iron Maiden was simply heavy metal. This made sense to me and I accepted his explanation. Not long after this there was a man by the name of Rob Mackenzie who had written a book by the name of 'Bands, Boppers, and Believers'. Whilst on a tour of all high schools in the country he made a stop at Plumtree and gave his presentation, in The Beit Hall, to the entire school. The presentation was a stark warning on the dangers and evils of heavy metal and the hidden messages within the music that were there to brainwash the listener. There was a visual presentation as well showing pictures of bands like Kiss, Led Zeppelin, Black Sabbath and Iron Maiden.

His message was clear and he said that this music was a medium through which Satan was consolidating his control over young people and manipulating them into a life of Devil worship. At one stage he played the song 'Another one bites the dust' by Queen backwards on a record player and claimed that listeners could hear the words 'It's fun to smoke Marijuana' in the chorus. Of course, this is ridiculous and it was very likely that the man was simply promoting his book. For us, his presentation had the complete opposite effect of what he had intended. A lot of the boys became and remain to this day, dedicated metal heads.

CHAPTER FOURTEEN

The Computer

For most boys, the arrival of the first ever computer at Plumtree School was of no interest at all. But for fellow Milner boy Ward and myself, this represented a major technological leap for us all and was very exciting. It had been decided by the school authorities that there would be a dedicated computer room and it would be situated next door to the art classroom near Wax Candler's house. A number of boys from other houses had expressed interest in the computer as well, and before long there were voluntary short courses in the afternoons so we could learn some rudimentary skills. If I recall correctly, the programming language was 'Basic' and it lived up to its name by being fairly easy to learn. Ward and I read up on computer articles in any magazines we could find and before long we had come up with an idea. Our plan was to create a computer game that could be played by anyone. Although we had no knowledge of how to create graphics, we had heard about certain adventure games where the player would find him or herself in a certain geographic location described in written word, and would then be given a series of three options on where to go next. The player would then indicate their choice by typing either A, B, or C and the game would progress to the next location. Of course, all of these adventure games had a goal or a prize at the end and once found or accomplished, the game would finish. Ward and I set about creating a huge chart of locations in the dark streets of an imaginary city. There were a series of gloomy alleys with shops, pubs, and various dangers in the form of rivers, knife wielding muggers and thieves. Players would even find themselves confronted by vicious dogs if they chose to travel down certain streets, but the ultimate goal was to find the girl. If players made the wrong choices, they would either find themselves back at the start of the game or they would be killed and would have to begin again. The design and structure of the game was written during evening prep over the course of a week until finally it was complete and the only thing left was to reproduce it on the old Apple computer.

This would be a laborious and time-consuming process but that was not the only issue. We were faced with a far more serious problem. The name of our adventure game masterpiece was 'Hunt The Whore'. Ward and I were more than aware that if we attempted to get the program on to the computer, our work would be instantly seen and flagged by the overzealous seniors who guarded the computer and literally watched over our shoulders whenever we were granted access to it. We realized that our work would have to go ahead after lights out and under cover of darkness. It was later that week when we first crept out of Milner House at 10.00 pm at night and made our way past the Beit Hall to the computer room. The window latch we had left slightly open swung easily and we climbed in, turned on the bright neon lights, and got to work. If I remember correctly it took around seven nocturnal visits to the computer room to complete the game and fully test it, but eventually it was done and it worked perfectly. We saved the game on a hard disc that we foolishly hid at the back of a drawer in the computer room. Sadly, within a few weeks the disc was found and our game discovered by the school authorities. Although we received no formal punishment, our parents were informed that we had secretly created a 'pornographic' computer game. In retrospect I don't think we did anything seriously wrong and apart from its name, it was nothing of the sort. I think that what we did was a fine work of innovation and creativity. Unfortunately, the game was deleted and Ward and I never returned to the computer room. I did hear that later in life, Ward had an extremely successful career in the computer business in Johannesburg South Africa. So, all in all, I guess it wasn't such a bad thing.

CHAPTER FIFTEEN

Busted

Saturday nights were eagerly anticipated by the entire school, given that there would be a movie screening in the Beit Hall. The film club were responsible for maintaining the projector and the screen and they would do their best to create an environment that felt similar to what one would experience when visiting a real cinema in any of the bigger cities. This included a 15 minute interval half way through the movie when the boys would congregate and mingle on the front steps of the Beit Hall. Smilie and I normally used this free time to sneak off for a cigarette and a favourite spot of ours to do this was the dark space behind the chapel. It was around that time that I became aware that a number of jock prefects and seniors in Milner House had focussed their attention on me. They would pick on me at any opportunity and as a result I was getting more than my fair share of weekly impots. Perhaps it was my growing confidence, the fact that I wasn't really into sport, or simply that they all knew I was a smoker. Either way, my strategy of avoiding them wasn't working as well as previously and I was fully aware there were knives out for me. It was one of those Saturday nights during the interval, when Smilie and I made our way across the basketball court, up the tarred road and into the darkness behind the chapel. We stood there in the moonlight and lit up our cigarettes while talking in hushed tones. We had no idea that a group of prefects had followed us from a distance and were getting ready to pounce. It was as we were about to extinguish our cigarettes that they suddenly sprang out of the darkness and grabbed us by our collars. After a thorough beating our cigarettes were impounded and we were told we would both be reported to our respective house masters. Smilie and I had been busted, and in grand style. The night was spent in deep worry about what the following day would bring. It was inevitable that we would both be given six of the best. It was well known that this was the standard punishment for boys caught smoking and it was for this reason that I put out the word that I was needing a 'bum pad'. A 'bum pad' was an ingenious piece of equipment that was handed around the school to boys who were in some kind of trouble and knew that they would be caned.

Fashioned from the rubber inner tube of a car tyre, it was cut in a figure of eight configuration similar to the size of the average buttocks, and had a small square hole cut into each side to allow for air flow and to help make the impact of the cane sound authentic. The word was sent out and the next morning a bum pad was delivered to my dormitory. On instructions from the other boys I stripped down to my underwear and put on another four pairs. I then fitted the bum pad between two pairs and proceeded to put on another three pairs. Suitably padded I waited for the inevitable summons to the office of the house master Harry West. It came before lunch time and I was told that as a result of being caught smoking I would be given six of the best. The cane was removed from an umbrella stand in the corner of the office and I was instructed to bend over with my hands on the desk. Thanks to the bum pad the beating was quick and fairly painless, but I noted a frown of concern on Harry's face afterwards. There was no doubt he knew that I was wearing it. Feeling happy it was over I walked back to the dormitory and removed the many layers of underwear. It was soon after, however, that I was called to the study of my chief persecutor, Williams, and told that I would be put on dress parade and 'stupa' for the next four weeks. Dress parade was a punishment that entailed wearing full blazer, tie, and longs during every waking moment. Added to that, boys on dress parade were made to stand in front of the top table at the graze hall as grace was said at every mealtime. 'Stupa' was another punishment which required the offender to carry a notebook everywhere which was to be signed on the hour, every waking hour of the day by either a teacher or a prefect. This added punishment, combined with dress parade, was a little over the top as far as I was concerned, and represented the growing dislike certain jock seniors had for me. One of the worst things about 'stupa' was the fact that I was to visit the prefect's common room once a day. Situated near the tuck shop, this was a feared place strictly reserved for prefects and any boy who wished to enter would have to call for permission three times from the gate.

"Come please, come please, come please!" I would shout every day before walking up the pathway and into what was literally the lions' den.

Depending on the mood of the prefects I would either be told to make them cups of tea and serve them or simply get punched in the chest and told to leave. One boy I know was told to put his hand on the dart board and ended up with a dart firmly embedded in his wrist. This combination of punishment was extreme and tedious but I continued to smoke during the duration. But one thing was clear. I would need to be more careful in future.

CHAPTER SIXTEEN

The Letter

It was just another normal day. I was on my way back to the dormitory at Milner House to drop my school bag off before heading down to the graze hall for lunch. It was as I was climbing the steps at the front of the house that a senior by the name of Constantino stopped me and spoke.

"Wallis," he said. "I heard your father died."

I stopped in my tracks and frowned at him.

"Excuse me, no," I replied using the abbreviation 'Sme'.

"Oh, okay," he said and went about his business, as did I.

It was as I was dropping my bag off that I saw the letter addressed to me lying on my bed. Knowing it would more than likely be from my parents I pocketed it deciding I would read it after lunch during rest. It was as I was walking out of the dormitory that I was stopped by the housemaster, Harry, and told to follow him into his residence at the rear of the building. I knew then there was something seriously wrong as this never ever happened. The fact that I had been asked the strange question by the senior minutes before confirmed this and it was with a sense of impending dread that I followed Harry into his lounge to find my younger brother sitting there as well. I was told to sit down next to him on the couch while Harry took a seat in front of us, his wife, Felix, stood nearby.

"Boys," he said, "I'm very sorry to tell you that your father has died."

The rush of emotions was harrowing, confusing, and frightening all at the same time. I recall being completely dumbstruck while my brother began crying and accusing Harry of lying.

Thankfully Felix came up and comforted us and we were eventually driven down to the hospital where we were told to wait. The matron, Mrs 'Ma' Meaden, kept an eye on us and the kitchen staff brought our lunch. My brother and I were too upset to eat and instead sat around in a state of shock. While we waited I opened the letter that I had folded and put in my top pocket only twenty minutes beforehand. I instantly recognised the handwriting as being that of my father's and given the circumstances I could only bring myself to read the last two lines he had written.

"Strive to be happy... Love Dad," it read.

This brought on a fresh wave of tears, but I said nothing and quickly put the letter back in the envelope and pocketed it once again. I could not bring myself to fully read that letter for many months, and I still have it to this day. Harry returned after two hours and told us we were to be driven to Bulawayo airport where we would catch the late afternoon flight to Harare. The long drive through the bush was spent in silence and eventually we arrived at the airport and boarded the plane. We were met on the apron of the runway at Harare by my mother and some family friends who took us home.

CHAPTER SEVENTEEN

The Big Heist

It was towards the end of my second year at the school. We had arranged a good table at the graze hall with an affable bunch of boys including the senior who was a 5th year by the name of McCallister. All of us got on well and actually enjoyed our mealtimes which was rare. One of the boys at the table was a fellow 4th year by the name of Biffo who was in the 1st team water polo team. We hadn't really noticed but he had been in an exceptionally good mood all week and being a naturally cheerful fellow, it was not unusual and we thought nothing of it. It was after dinner on a Friday when most of the boys, including Biffo, had finished eating and were making their way back to their respective houses that we first heard the whispered news of the recent robbery in the village. The news came from McCallister who relayed the story in a very matter of fact way. There had been a robbery earlier in the week in the village at Costello's Store and a large amount of alcohol had been stolen. It was suspected that Plumtree boys were involved although there was no other information. Costello's was a Greek owned store near the school gates and a lot of boys would visit to buy sweets and supplies. It was also the largest bottle store in Plumtree and being a border town it stocked the much coveted imported brands which were difficult to find at the time. Of course none of the boys would ever attempt to purchase cigarettes or alcohol there as the owners were well known to the school authorities, but it seemed their large stocks of booze had not gone unnoticed. This news was of great interest to the four boys, including myself, who remained chatting at our table. After much discussion it was decided that we would attempt to find the illicit stash the following day. We were fully aware that it was a long shot, and it was possible that the robbery had absolutely nothing to do with any boys from the school, but we were willing to give it a try. Given the strict rules about fraternising with juniors, it would have been improper for McCallister to join us in the search, so it was decided that three of us would meet the following day to start looking. Before we left the table it was agreed that our endeavour should remain secret and that nothing was to be said to anyone else from that moment onwards. That night I lay awake wondering exactly what had been stolen, who was responsible, and thinking through the many possible locations that the loot might have been hidden.

It was after prep the next day that the three of us met near the armoury and began our search. All of us had a number of suggestions that needed to be thoroughly investigated and so began an exhausting day of climbing, crawling, and sneaking into every nook and cranny we could think of throughout the entire school. We climbed into the attic of the cricket pavilion followed by the vast spaces above and below the Beit Hall. We searched through the storage sheds of each house, rummaging beneath piles of old garden machinery, wooden crates and tarpaulins. We scoured the entire perimeter of the school looking for signs of disturbed earth where something might have been freshly buried. We went into each and every classroom of the school quadrangle, found the trapdoors in the wooden floors, and went below into the darkness on all fours using candles as we crawled around. Our search was so extensive that we missed lunch that Saturday instead staying focussed on our quarry. But sadly it all came to nothing and it was at around 4.00 pm that we all sat down to discuss the next step. A few of the boys had lost heart by then but we agreed that we would apply for bush exits and continue the search the following day outside the grounds of the school. We were, after all, completely in the dark as to what exactly had been stolen if anything and even then if it was Plumtree boys who were responsible. It was with heavy hearts and filthy clothes that we took the long walk past the chapel towards our respective houses for shower time, roll call, and dinner. It was then that one of us noticed the school library to our left. The ancient red brick building stood in the shadows of a huge fig tree. Like most of the old school buildings it had been fitted with the occasional small ceramic air vent around the base of the structure to allow its foundations to breathe. One of these air vents at the left corner of the building was broken leaving a tiny dark hole that was obscured by the scraggy surrounding grass.

"Shall we take a look?" asked Bailey.

With exhausted sighs we trudged up to the old building and got down on our hands and knees to peer into the dark foundations of the building.

"There's something there," I whispered excitedly, as my eyes adjusted to the gloom.

"What can you see Wally?" urged someone.

It took some seconds for the words on the box to become clear, but it was with great excitement that I read them out aloud.

"Johnny Walker, Red Label," I cried out in disbelief. "Product of Scotland."

Suddenly the weariness and disappointment of the day evaporated and was instantly replaced by a buzzing excitement as we all jostled for a peek. There were a number of boxes in there although most of them could not be seen. A hurried conference was held where it was decided we would tell no-one except McCallister and that we would finalise our plans during the interval of the movie later that night. We all headed off to our respective houses to shower and then walk down to the graze hall. The urge to talk about our discovery at dinner was desperate but we held our resolve until everyone at the table had left barring McCallister. We blurted out the news in hushed voices telling him of the exhaustive search, the sheer ingenuity of the hiding place, and the joy of our discovery. We still had absolutely no idea who had done the initial heist but we were now in a position to take the prize from them. It was shaping up to be the biggest coup of our lives. A tentative plan was made to camouflage ourselves and meet at the rising bell after lights out at 11.00 pm. This was confirmed later during the interval of the Saturday night movie. That night I lay awake as the other boys in the dorm fell asleep.

At around 10.45 pm I changed into my dark green tracksuit, blackened my face with shoe polish, and slipped silently out of Milner House for the short walk down to the rising bell. The other three boys, including McCallister, arrived soon after and we all headed up to the library. It took some time to get in as the door was locked but eventually we found a window that had been left partially open.

We all climbed into the dark interior of the library, lit our candles, and began searching for a trapdoor in the polished wooden floor. We found it hidden in the centre of the room under a heavy desk and proceeded to open it and climb down into the bowels of the old building. Crawling on all fours, with candles in hands, we made our way towards where we knew the stash to be hidden. What we didn't know was that the foundations of the building had been segmented by bricked support walls and we soon came to a dead end. We crawled back and forth desperately searching for an access point but it was to no avail. The illicit haul was within metres but we were unable to get to it. Eventually, feeling flummoxed, we climbed out, closed the trapdoor and regrouped. Determined not to be beaten, we walked to the far corner of the library to the point where we knew the stash to lie beneath. There was a large pile of antique cabinet scales stacked up in the corner and we formed a human chain as we began to carefully shift them. After some time and effort we had them moved and we finally saw what we were expecting. In the floor at the centre of where the scales had been stacked was a trap door.

"This has to be it!" said one of the boys.

Candles in hand, we crouched down and lifted the recessed brass ring of the trapdoor. There was a combined sharp intake of breath as what lay below was finally revealed in the yellow glow of the candles. Boxes upon boxes, crates upon crates of Scotch whisky, brandy, cane spirit and vodka. There was no doubt, we had hit the mother lode.

Bailey climbed down and began lifting the boxes out one by one. Once done we closed the trapdoor and began the laborious task of replacing the cabinet scales in the corner of the room. Next, we formed another chain and shifted the crates out of the window and on to the grass outside. With all the boys out and the window closed, a hurried conference was held in the darkness under the fig tree to decide on our next move.

With the security fence that marked the boundary of the school grounds being just beyond the chapel it was decided that we would move the haul out of the school grounds and into the bush beyond. It took two or three trips to move them all to the fence and then began the process of lifting them over the barbed wire. Once finished we walked down the railway tracks in the moonlight for half a kilometre until we found a suitable bush in which to hide them. It must have been around 3.30 am by the time we all made it back to our respective houses and lay down to sleep. That morning after breakfast we convened another meeting to plot the way forward. Although the hiding place we had chosen was good, it would only be a matter of time until it was discovered by a wandering member of the public. The obvious choice was the old man from the village in Tegwani who had sold us the home brewed beer but getting it there posed a big problem as it was at least 10 km away. One of us came up with a solution involving a day scholar by the name of Ross whose parents lived in the village. This boy had a driving licence and was known to have the use of an old open top Land Rover. One of the boys got a bush exit and went to visit the day scholar in the village to see if it was possible to move them. He returned an hour later saying it had been arranged and that we would all meet near the railway tracks at 2.00 pm. The four of us arrived at the meeting point early and waited anxiously for Ross to arrive. Eventually we saw the dust of the approaching vehicle and we all climbed in for the drive down the railway tracks to our hiding spot. We arrived to find the loot undisturbed and quickly loaded it into the vehicle then covered it with an old tarpaulin. The drive down the dirt road to Tegwani was quick and the old man was surprised to see five boys trundling up to his village in a Land Rover.

After a quick discussion the crates were loaded into his hut and we told him he was free to drink as much of the brandy as he liked in return for allowing us to store it there. This pleased him no end and we left after telling him we would return later in the week. That evening the four of us went dinner glowing with what we thought was an astounding achievement. Once again, we were resolute in our non-disclosure rule and said nothing of it until the rest of the table had left.

What we didn't notice, however, was the fact that our friend from the 1st team water polo team, Biffo, was inexplicably glum. There was a very good reason for this that we would only find out much later. With the half term exeat looming the following weekend, we started making plans on how we would smuggle some of it home on the bus. Bailey came up with the novel idea of removing the batteries from a large ghetto blaster and placing a bottle of whisky inside. The rest of decided we would simply put a couple of bottles in our bags and board the bus as usual. Later that week we took the long walk out to Tegwani to retrieve some of the loot. The old man was in fine spirits and we all returned to the school that afternoon carrying what we thought we would need for the weekend at home. The week was spent in a state of excited anticipation of the coming weekend at home but once again, no-one at the table noticed the fact that Biffo seemed to be somewhat down in the dumps. On the morning we were due to leave we all packed our bags and made our way to where the bus waited near the basketball court. It was only when we arrived there that we saw that each and every boy was being subjected to a thorough search by a group of teachers as they entered the bus. It was clear then that they knew full well that it had been schoolboys who had robbed Costello's store although they had no idea of the bizarre series of events that had followed. Bailey took the lead and walked on board the bus carrying his tape deck with the bottle of whisky in the battery compartment. The teachers never gave it a second look and he boarded without any problems. Having to think on our feet, the rest of us quickly walked around to the other side of the bus where we stealthily handed our bags to Bailey through an open window.

He quickly unloaded the bottles into his own bag and threw ours back out to us.

With the search not turning up anything, the bus left the school grounds and we were finally on our way home with our illicit cargo. We arrived in Harare some seven hours later and wasted no time selling the valuable and coveted scotch whisky to our friends' parents. We did, of course, keep some brandy for the following night where our plan was to meet at the Flagstaff Bar in Meikles Hotel. Frequented by Plumtree boys, there was also the Causerie Night Club in the same building where we knew there would be girls.

So it was with pockets full of money and a bottle of brandy hidden in a nearby flower bed that we spent the evening at the hotel before returning home in the early hours of Sunday morning in a Renault 4 Rixi Taxi. Having all had an excellent weekend we happily boarded the bus early the following Monday morning and began the long drive back to Plumtree School. We felt like we were on top of our game, invincible even. But it was only when we arrived back at the school that dark clouds started gathering and everything fell apart. It turned out that the day scholar who had helped us move the goods to Tegwani had spent the exeat weekend with the son of the school art teacher in Plumtree village. I'm not sure whether they had been caught drinking or perhaps they had been pressured for information by their parents, but the cat was well and truly out of the bag and we were in serious trouble. Not only had our own house of cards collapsed but the boys who had done the initial heist had been rumbled as well. It turned out that it had been a group of boys from the 1st team water polo squad. They had gone into the village at night, waited for a goods train to pass, and used the noise to cover the sound of them opening the back doors of Costello's Store with a crowbar. They had gone to great lengths to find and secure their hiding place only to have their stash stolen once again by us. Finally, we realised why Biffo had been so down in the dumps the previous week. We had been sitting at the very same table as one of the boys who had conducted the initial heist and neither of us had been aware of the activities of the others. The water polo boys were all expelled immediately whilst we were made to wait to discover our fate. Although the whole saga was kept quiet and no police were called, our parents were made to pay the replacement costs of the missing booze. This was a substantial amount and there was even more trouble to come. It was only after the water polo team had left the school that it was time for our group of secondary criminals to receive our punishment. The summons to the headmaster's office came suddenly and I had no time to arrange a bum pad. With a sense of extreme dread I took the long walk past the Beit Hall up to the administration block where Spike waited. The tall man was extremely angry and chose an extra thick cane for my punishment. The slow beating of six of the best was the most painful of my life and left me with raised, angry purple welts on my backside.

Once again, I found myself on dress parade although this time, I was thankfully not given the extra punishment of Stupa. The event sent shock waves through the school and somehow changed everything for me. Given the fact that we were not involved in the initial heist we were spared the humiliation of being expelled. Our crime was not deemed as serious as the initial one. But for me, something had changed, and I felt given the circumstances I could no longer stay at the school. It was within a few days that I approached our house master, Harry, and asked to leave. Given the recent events my request was quickly granted and my parents were informed. Within a few days I was collected by my parents and I left Plumtree School for good.

CHAPTER EIGHTEEN

School's Out

Although I was initially happy to get home, it was a strange and bittersweet moment for me. Only then did I realise that I had left a lot of good friends at Plumtree School and my future was now uncertain. Gone were the strict routines and rules that I had become so accustomed to. Gone was the constant game of cat and mouse with the seniors and teachers who were out to get me. There would be no more bush exits, no more army games, and no more laughter and fun at the graze hall and in the dormitories. It came as a surprise that I found myself missing the camaraderie and the regulations that I had become so used to. My parents had enrolled me in a college in Harare where there were no uniforms and basically no rules. Coming from such a strict institution I found it extremely hard to fit in. I soon found that life in Harare was boring and empty and I truly missed the school even with all its hardships. It was towards the end of the term that a Harare friend and I hitch hiked to Bulawayo for a night ostensibly to see a friend of mine. In reality I knew the boys from my old school would be on their way home for the holidays the following day and I wanted to catch the Plumtree bus one final time. We caught a lift early in the morning from Bulawayo to the small town of

Gweru. The driver was fully prepared to take us all the way to Harare as he was going there anyway, but I thanked him and refused. We waited patiently at the Midlands Hotel until the familiar old green bus with the red stripe pulled in filled with cheerful boys on their way home for the holidays. My friends were surprised to see me and I boarded the bus for one last journey to Harare. I will never forget my time at that school far away in the bush on the border with Botswana. A school that for all its faults, turned boys into gentlemen and instilled in its students good values, discipline and a healthy respect for their elders. A school steeped in rich history and tradition. Plumtree School.

The End.

Printed in Great Britain
by Amazon